Why Do We Celebrate Evacuation Day?

by the students, parents, and teachers of the

Michael J. Perkins School

Boston, Massachusetts

Third Edition – March 2009

a project of

The Entrepreneurial Public School™

Can you imagine that there was a battle with almost no blood – just victory for the Americans?

This amazing victory happened in 1776 right behind our school, in the neighborhood that is now called South Boston. In 1776, our school was not built yet, and back then South Boston was called Dorchester Heights.

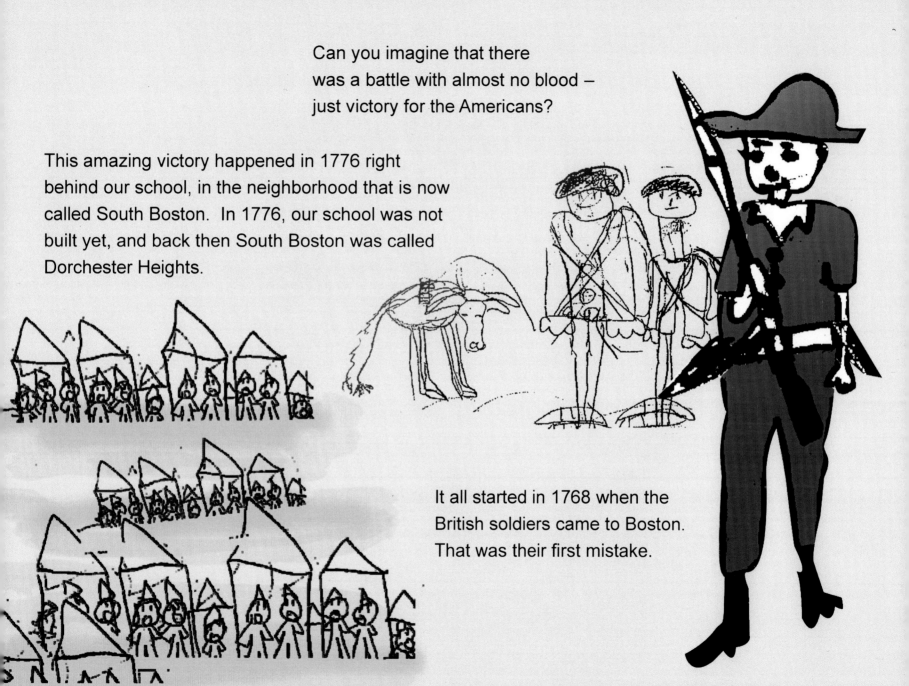

It all started in 1768 when the British soldiers came to Boston. That was their first mistake.

People in Boston were mad because the British raised up taxes.
The colonists did not have enough money because the British kept
on taking the money. The colonists had to pay extra taxes on glass,
paints, and tea.

The British soldiers were sent to Boston to make the colonists
pay those taxes.

If you had a house and the British wanted soldiers to sleep there, you had to do it.
Sometimes British soldiers took jobs from hard-working Bostonians. One of the mean, vicious
things the British did was they used the colonists' churches to keep their horses in, like a stable.
The British even broke down houses just to get firewood.

People in Boston were mad.
They wanted the British soldiers to leave.

On March 5, 1770, British soldiers shot into an angry crowd

and killed colonists at the Boston Massacre.

That made the colonists even madder.

The Americans had a fort they built in the Charlestown part of Boston. In June, 1775, there was a terrible battle in Charlestown near Bunker Hill. British ships started shooting at the Americans in Charlestown. Hundreds of British soldiers landed in boats and started going up the hill.

Because Americans didn't have many bullets, Colonel Prescott, their leader, said not to shoot until you could see the whites in the enemy's eyes. So they were shooting very close up. It was a horrible, horrible, battle. By the time the fighting was over, the British won – but so many British soldiers and Americans were killed that neither side wanted to do it again.

In July, 1775, General George Washington came to Cambridge, across the Charles River from Boston, to be the leader of the colonists' army.

The colonists did not have much guns or ammunition, and many of their soldiers were sick.

The colonists were all around Boston, and the British were still <u>in</u> Boston.

The British had guns and ships, but they did not have much food.

They didn't have much firewood to keep them warm when the weather got cold.

Neither side knew what to do next.

Then Henry Knox had a brilliant idea. Henry Knox was a young man who was a soldier with the colonists. He used to own a bookstore in Boston, and he read many books about guns, battles, and wars. He knew there were lots of cannons at Fort Ticonderoga in New York State.

The Americans had just taken Fort Ticonderoga away from the British.

Henry Knox asked General George Washington if he could go to Fort Ticonderoga to get the cannons and bring them to Boston to fight the British. The cannons were more than 300 miles away, and they were very heavy.

General Washington said,

"Yes. Do it."

Henry
Knox

9

Henry Knox and his men traveled to Fort Ticonderoga and got more than 50 big cannons there.

Some of the cannons weighed 2,000 pounds each or even 5,000 pounds for each one.

All together, the cannons weighed 119,000 pounds.

It was like taking ten Tyrannosaurus Rexes to weigh as much as those 50 cannons.

They had to take the cannons 32 miles to Lake George. Then they had to load the cannons onto boats called "scows". The boats almost sank with the heavy cannons. They had to battle headwinds and row the boats in the freezing cold.

It took eight days just to travel across Lake George.

Then they made sleds to take the cannons across the land. They got oxen and hooked up reins on the oxen to pull the sleds. First, the weather was warm and there was no snow for the sleds to slide on. Then there was a blizzard with too much snow for them to travel.

Finally, they got moving again.

When they had to take the cannons across the Hudson River, they were worried the ice was not strong enough to hold them up. Henry Knox did something smart. He had the soldiers cut holes in the ice. Then water would rise up and freeze and the ice would get thicker and thicker, so the cannons would not fall. But one fell.

They still didn't give up. They pulled the cannon up and cleaned it, then kept on moving.

Imagine you had to carry 119,000 pounds of cannons and get them up and down the hills called the Berkshire Mountains.

When the men said, "General Knox, we cannot do this. It is too heavy," he would tell them, "You are halfway there. Don't turn your back on me."

The British did not know the cannons were coming because the British were far away in Boston. There were no telephones or televisions back then. The only way people could communicate was by getting on a horse and going to a place to see what was happening. Or you could send a letter that someone else took on a horse or ship. The British were stuck in Boston, with colonists all around them. They did not know the colonists were bringing all those cannons.

Henry Knox – with the help of hundreds of men, oxen, and horses – finally got the cannons to the town of Framingham, which is about 20 miles west of Boston. They stopped there. Henry Knox rode to Cambridge to talk with George Washington. General Washington had to decide how to use the cannons to attack the British in Boston.

They decided on a spectacular plan.

They would sneak the cannons up to the top of Dorchester Heights in one night,
so the British would not see them until it was too late.
The Americans would also get lots of barrels and fill them with rocks.

If the British troops tried to go up Dorchester Heights,
the colonists would drop the barrels on them and
the British would just get smashed.

General Washington decided to do all this in one night, March 5, 1776 – the same date that British soldiers killed colonists at the Boston Massacre, six years before. They would surprise the British.

Several thousand men had to work all through the night, with oxen and horses, to get the cannons to the top of Dorchester Heights, which was 112 feet high.

The next day when the British woke up and saw all of the cannons on the hill, they couldn't believe their eyes.

19

When the British woke up, they saw the cannons on Dorchester Heights.
The British General Howe said, "Let's fight!",

but that was their last mistake.

The British soldiers said, "Why?" "No way!" and "You're crazy!" The British cannons could not shoot all the way to the top of Dorchester Heights, but the colonists' cannons could shoot down. Also, the colonists had all those barrels filled with rocks.

General Howe sent for ships to come across Boston Harbor to Castle Island near Dorchester Heights. He wanted to bring guns and knives and more cannons for a big battle with the colonists.

As the British ships tried to sail, a huge storm came out of nowhere. The winds and snow were so strong they broke windows in Boston.

The storm blew the ships off course, and they couldn't get to Castle Island. General Howe gave up his plan to attack. Instead, the British decided to get all their soldiers and friends, get on their boats, and leave Boston.

They were going to "evacuate" (which means to "make empty" or "withdraw") from Boston.

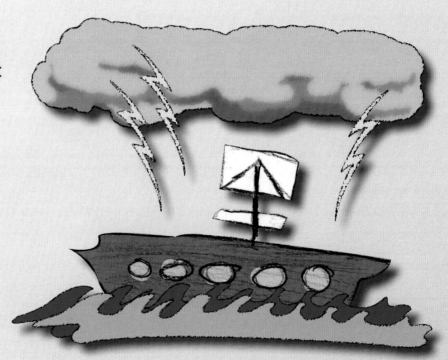

As they were leaving, the British told the people of Boston to stay in their homes and not to get in their way. They needed 120 ships to carry all the people, including over 8,000 soldiers and thousands of women, children, and people who were called "Loyalists" because they wanted to be loyal to (that is, stay with) Great Britain and King George.

British soldiers broke into houses and shops and stole food to take on their trip. They also stole valuable supplies. When the British finally left on March 17, 1776 – Evacuation Day – they left a lot of destruction in Boston.

But the British soldiers left without a fight.
It was good for the Americans.
The colonists were really, really happy.
"Victory! Hurray!" screamed the people.

Do you know why?
It was because the cruel, mean, vicious British
and their soldiers had left Boston.

Evacuation Day was George Washington's proudest moment of the war, so far.

It was the colonists' first victory in the Revolutionary War, also called the War of Independence. America became independent of Britain and started our own country.

Why do we celebrate Evacuation Day?

We celebrate Evacuation Day because it was a victory with almost no blood!

We celebrate Evacuation Day because the British soldiers had taken over Boston. When they left, the Americans could be in charge of our own city. Now people could make their own laws and stand for their own rights!

We celebrate Evacuation Day because one clever idea – and a lot of hard work – can change history!

Even though some people think we celebrate March 17 only for St. Patrick's Day
(which also happens on March 17),

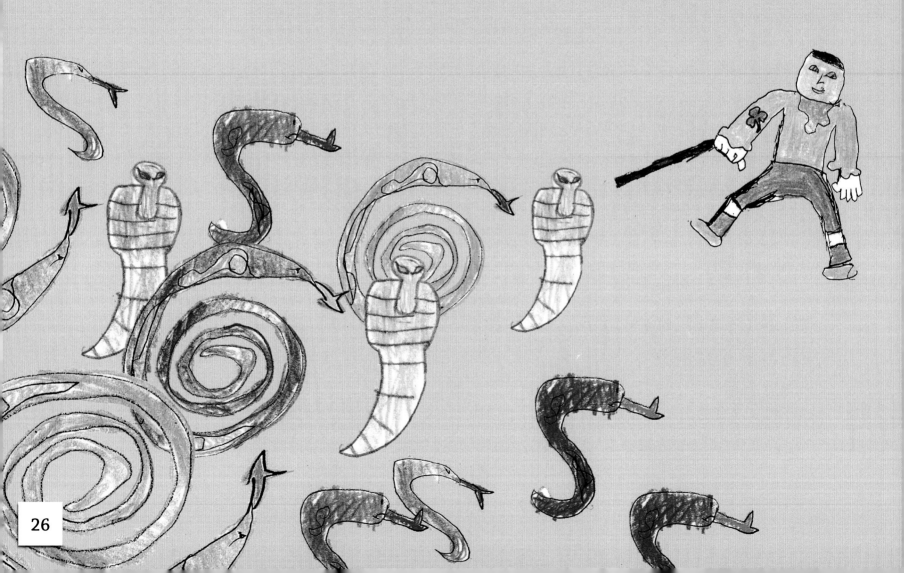

we know that Evacuation Day was a <u>real</u> holiday, since the beginning of our country's history –

and it happened right behind our school!

We thank all the people who helped us write, illustrate, publish, and sell this Third Edition of

Why Do We Celebrate Evacuation Day?

We especially thank our

authors and illustrators

Matthew Bergeron	Justin Louis	Idrese Soares
Dimera Capel Wideman	Austin Martin	Cassandra St.Germain
Isriah Cotton	Isaiah Martinez	Nico Suarez
Sammy Cruz-Moreta	Nicole Martinez	Steven Suero
Jacob DePina	Desmond McCaskill	Tanaiah Sweet
Tiana Dickinson	Adelajda Mullahi	Xavier Thompson
Shanna-Kay Fagan	Cindy Nguyen	Dionis Torres
Shawn Fleurime	Jackie Nguyen	Long Tran
Alyssa Furkart	Edgard Nieves	Andy Truong
Semaj Harris	Mohamed Noor	Kaijahna Tyson
Jose Hernandez	Maria Pimentel	Edwin Vallejo
Faiso Hersi	Angel Prats-Diaz	Edgard Walker
Khadija Ibrahim	Clevan Richards	Tamari Washington
Rashea Ivey-Lewis	Natalie Rosario	Londyn Webb
Elhan Jama	Nicholas Rose	Eddy Vasquez
Shameka Joseph	Ireidys Santana	Ramon Vega
Robert Juliano	Alani Santos	La'Lonnie Witkowski
Amber Lentini	Amira Sharifnur	Ms. Stevens' 06-07 kindergarten class
Judah Leslie	Andre Smith	

helpful grown-ups

Marcia Russell, Jan Goedeke, Alana McDonough, and Felicia Brown
Harvard Graduate School of Education

Derek Nelson
Theatre Espresso

Jerry and Linda Paros

Sidewalk Sam and Chris Montecalvo
Art Street, Inc.

Chobee Hoy Associates Real Estate, Inc.
Brookline, MA

Virginia Yazbeck
Perkins School Art Teacher

Glenda Clark
Perkins School Parent

Harvard Book Store
Massachusetts Avenue, Cambridge, MA

FedEx Kinko's Store # 0500
Beacon Street, Brookline, MA

Amy Couch
Production/Layout Designer

Charlie P. Mooney
Ames On-Demand Printers, Somerville, MA

and the entire Michael J. Perkins School community.

Honor the past. Build the future.

The Michael J. Perkins School, built in 1926, is a Boston public elementary school, grades K – 5.

Our **College Scholarship Fund** helps our graduating fifth graders and their families make a personal commitment, prepare academically, and begin to save financially for a successful college education.

Michael J. Perkins School

50 Burke Street

South Boston, MA 02127

(617) 635 – 8601